Bob woke up and yawned. He hadn't slept well in weeks. Bob slowly got out of bed and rolled to the kitchen. His father had made him breakfast but Bob wasn't hungry. He skipped breakfast and headed off to school. Bob rolled the whole way.

Normally Bob would bounce up and down every street until he reached the school gate but today he didn't feel like it. As a matter of fact, Bob had rolled to school every day for the last two weeks. Bob had lost his bounce.

When Bob arrived at school he saw his
friends.
"Come and play handball," they said.
"No thanks," replied Bob. "I'm too tired."
"We could play soccer instead," suggested
Bob's friends.
"No!" said Bob. "I just want to be left
alone!"

Bob didn't have a good day at school. No matter how hard he tried, he just couldn't concentrate. During basketball, he had trouble bouncing. During netball, he had trouble bouncing. During football, he had trouble bouncing. Normally, Bob was a great bouncer.

"What's wrong?" asked Bob's teacher.

"I'm useless," said Bob. "I can't do anything right."

The next day, Bob woke up and yawned.
He skipped breakfast again and rolled to
school. Waiting at the school gate was his
best friend.

"How are you Bob?" asked Boomer. Bob
wiped the tears from his eyes.

"I feel flat," said Bob. "I'm not flat on the
outside but I feel flat and sad on the
inside."

"Why do you feel sad?" asked Boomer.

"That's the problem," said Bob. "I don't

know."

Bob was confused. He didn't understand why he was always sad. He had a caring family who loved him. He had great friends who played with him. He did well at school and was an excellent bouncer. He shouldn't have a worry in the world. Why wasn't he happy?

Boomer gave Bob a smile because smiles always seem to help.

"Everyone gets sad," said Boomer. "We all have sad days now and again."

"But I've been sad for weeks," explained Bob.

"Well, that's different then," said Boomer. "You need to talk to a grown up about this so that they can find someone to help you."

Bob took Boomer's advice. He talked to his parents and told them how he felt. His parents took Bob to a doctor. The doctor said that Bob wasn't just flat - he was deflated. The doctor said that some people call this *depression*. Bob felt a little better. He was going to get the help he needed. It might take a while, but he would eventually get his bounce back.

Bob woke up after a good night's sleep. He bounced out of bed and ate a healthy breakfast. Bob gave his parents a hug and then bounced all the way to school. His bounce was not quite as high as normal but it was getting a little higher each day.

"Come and play handball," said Bob's
friends.
"You bet," said Bob with a laugh. Bob
played handball and soccer and bounced
with his friends. He bounced high in all his
lessons. When school was over for the day,
he even bounced all the way back home.

"What's new Boomer?" asked Bob.
"They're forming a new school volleyball team," explained Boomer. "Maybe we could try out."
"I don't know how to play volleyball," said Bob. "I'm good at bouncing but you're not allowed to bounce in volleyball."
"We could learn how to play," suggested Boomer.
"Let's give it a go," said Bob. "It might be fun."

Weeks later, Bob woke up and smiled. He'd had a great night's sleep. However, as he bounced to school, Bob was worried about not making the volleyball team. Then he remembered that it was important not to worry too much about the future. Bob thought about the present. He listened to the birds chirping in the trees. He waved to Mr Dribble who was sitting on his verandah. Bob then noticed that he was bouncing as high as ever.

Boomer met Bob at the school gate.
"How are you today Bob?"
"I'm pumped," said Bob. "You're a good
friend Boomer. You helped me get my
bounce back."
"That's what friends are for," replied
Boomer.
Bob and Boomer both smiled.

Activities

Talk about what these images are telling you about the story.

Activities

Talk about what these images are telling you about the story.

Activities

Talk about what these images are telling you about the story.

Activities

Talk about what these images are telling you about the story.